Breaking the Habit of Being Yourself

THE WORKBOOK

Disclaimer:

By using this workbook, you acknowledge and agree to the following terms. The information provided in this workbook is for educational purposes only and is not professional advice. Individual responsibility is crucial when applying the techniques and exercises, as results may vary. Consult a qualified professional before implementing any techniques if you have pre-existing medical or mental health conditions. We cannot guarantee specific outcomes, and this workbook is not a substitute for professional treatment. External resources mentioned are for informational purposes only, and we do not endorse their content. The workbook's content is protected by copyright, and personal liability lies with the user. By using this workbook, you release the creators and authors from any liability. Seek professional guidance and consider your circumstances and limitations. Consult a qualified professional before making any changes to your habits, thoughts, or behaviors.

Thank you for choosing to engage with this book. We hope it helps you build a healthy and loving relationship with your partner.

LESSONS IN THIS WORKBOOK:

1. The Habit of Being Yourself

2. Breaking the Habit

3. Your Brain on Change

4. Meditation: Changing Your Mind and Brain

5. Deciding Who to Be

6. Mind and Body

7. Overcoming Your Environment and Body

8. Entering the Quantum Field

9. Tuning in to New Potentials

Chapter 1:
The Habit of Being Yourself

Lesson 1:

Our thoughts, emotions, and behaviors form habitual patterns that shape our reality.

Take some time to reflect on your own habitual patterns of thinking, feeling, and behaving. Write down three specific patterns that you have noticed and how they have influenced your reality. Consider both positive and negative patterns.

_____

_____

_____

_____

_____

_____

_____

_____

_____

_____

_____

_____

_____

_____

_____

_____

_____

_____

_____

_____

_____

_____

_____

_____

_____

Choose one negative thought pattern that you would like to change. Write down three alternative, more empowering thoughts that you can replace it with. Reflect on how adopting these new thoughts can shape your reality in a more positive way.

_____

_____

_____

_____

_____

_____

_____

_____

_____

_____

_____

_____

_____

_____

_____

_____

_____

_____

_____

_____

_____

_____

_____

Imagine your ideal reality in terms of your thoughts, emotions, and behaviors. Write a detailed description of what it looks and feels like. Consider how aligning your current patterns with this ideal reality can create positive change.

_____

_____

_____

_____

_____

_____

_____

_____

_____

_____

_____

_____

_____

_____

_____

_____

_____

_____

_____

_____

_____

_____

_____

_____

_____

_____

_____

_____

Lesson 2:

To create meaningful change, we must break free from the habit of being our current selves.

Reflect on a specific area of your life where you feel stuck or stag-
nant. Write down three reasons why you believe you are holding
onto your current self and resisting change in that area.

Identify one small action or behavior that you can change today to start breaking free from your current self. Write down the action and its potential impact on your life. Reflect on the courage and willingness it requires to take that step.

_____

_____

_____

_____

_____

_____

_____

_____

_____

_____

_____

_____

_____

_____

_____

_____

_____

_____

_____

_____

_____

_____

Write a letter to your current self, expressing your desire for growth and change. Write down three reasons why embracing change and breaking free from your current self is essential for your personal development and fulfillment.

_____

_____

_____

_____

_____

_____

_____

_____

_____

_____

_____

_____

_____

_____

_____

_____

_____

_____

_____

_____

_____

_____

_____

Lesson 3:

By rewiring our brain and cultivating new thought patterns, we can create a new reality.

Reflect on a past experience where you successfully rewired a negative thought pattern. Write down the steps you took to challenge and replace that pattern with a more positive one. Reflect on how this shift in thought influenced your reality.

_____

_____

_____

_____

_____

_____

_____

_____

_____

_____

_____

_____

_____

_____

_____

_____

_____

_____

_____

_____

_____

_____

_____

_____

_____

Choose a specific negative thought pattern that you would like to rewire. Write down three affirmations or positive statements that counteract that pattern. Commit to repeating these affirmations daily and reflect on the changes you observe over time.

_____

_____

_____

_____

_____

_____

_____

_____

_____

_____

_____

_____

_____

_____

_____

_____

_____

_____

_____

_____

_____

_____

Create a vision board or visualization exercise that represents your desired new reality. Write a description of your vision board or visualization practice and how it aligns with your goal of rewiring your brain. Reflect on how regularly engaging with this practice can manifest positive changes in your reality.

_____

_____

_____

_____

_____

_____

_____

_____

_____

_____

_____

_____

_____

_____

_____

_____

_____

_____

_____

_____

_____

_____

_____

Chapter 2:
Breaking the Habit

Lesson 1:

Our brain's neural pathways create and reinforce our habits.

Reflect on a specific habit that you would like to break. Write down the triggers, actions, and rewards associated with that habit. Analyze how these components contribute to the reinforcement of the habit.

_____

_____

_____

_____

_____

_____

_____

_____

_____

_____

_____

_____

_____

_____

_____

_____

_____

_____

_____

_____

_____

_____

_____

_____

_____

Identify three alternative actions or behaviors that you can replace the old habit with. Write them down and describe how they can provide similar rewards or benefits.

_____

_____

_____

_____

_____

_____

_____

_____

_____

_____

_____

_____

_____

_____

_____

_____

_____

_____

_____

_____

_____

_____

_____

_____

_____

_____

Create a habit tracking journal. Write down the days and times when you engage in the old habit, along with any thoughts or emotions associated with it. Reflect on patterns and triggers that can help you understand the habit better.

Lesson 2:

Intentional and sustained focus on new thoughts and behaviors can rewire these neural pathways.

Choose one specific new thought or behavior that you want to cultivate. Write down three affirmations or positive statements related to that new thought or behavior. Commit to repeating these affirmations daily to reinforce the new pathway.

Write a letter to your future self, describing how your life will be transformed once you have successfully rewired your neural pathways. Be specific about the changes you envision and how they will positively impact your well-being.

_____

_____

_____

_____

_____

_____

_____

_____

_____

_____

_____

_____

_____

_____

_____

_____

_____

_____

_____

_____

_____

_____

_____

_____

Create a daily practice of mindfulness or meditation. Write down the specific techniques or exercises you will engage in to focus your attention on the present moment and reinforce new thought patterns.

_____

_____

_____

_____

_____

_____

_____

_____

_____

_____

_____

_____

_____

_____

_____

_____

_____

_____

_____

_____

_____

_____

_____

_____

_____

Lesson 3:

Breaking old habits requires consistency, commitment, and rewiring at both the conscious and subconscious levels.

Reflect on your level of commitment to breaking the old habit. Write down three reasons why breaking this habit is important to you and how it aligns with your long-term goals or values.

_____

_____

_____

_____

_____

_____

_____

_____

_____

_____

_____

_____

_____

_____

_____

_____

_____

_____

_____

_____

_____

_____

_____

_____

_____

Create a plan for consistent action. Write down three actionable steps you can take daily or weekly to reinforce the new habit and weaken the old habit. Set reminders and create accountability measures to stay on track.

_____

_____

_____

_____

_____

_____

_____

_____

_____

_____

_____

_____

_____

_____

_____

_____

_____

_____

_____

_____

_____

_____

_____

Use journaling as a tool to explore the subconscious beliefs or emotions associated with the old habit. Write freely about any underlying fears, doubts, or resistance you may have. Reflect on how addressing these subconscious aspects can support your habit-breaking journey.

_____

_____

_____

_____

_____

_____

_____

_____

_____

_____

_____

_____

_____

_____

_____

_____

_____

_____

_____

_____

_____

_____

_____

_____

Chapter 3:
Your Brain on Change

Lesson 1:

The brain is constantly evolving and capable of forming new neural connections throughout life.

Reflect on a time when you experienced personal growth or acquired a new skill. Write down the specific changes you observed in your thoughts, behaviors, and abilities. Consider how these changes reflect the brain's capacity for adaptation and rewiring.

_____

_____

_____

_____

_____

_____

_____

_____

_____

_____

_____

_____

_____

_____

_____

_____

_____

_____

_____

_____

_____

_____

_____

_____

_____

_____

_____

Choose one area of your life where you would like to see positive change. Write down three new experiences, activities, or knowledge that you can introduce to stimulate your brain's growth and formation of new neural connections.

_____

_____

_____

_____

_____

_____

_____

_____

_____

_____

_____

_____

_____

_____

_____

_____

_____

_____

_____

_____

_____

_____

_____

_____

_____

_____

_____

Create a "brain-boosting" routine. Write down three daily activities that engage different cognitive functions, such as reading, learning a musical instrument, or solving puzzles. Reflect on how these activities can support neuroplasticity and positive change.

Lesson 2:

By engaging in focused attention and visualization exercises, we can reprogram our neural circuitry.

Choose a specific aspect of your life that you would like to change or improve. Write down a detailed description of your desired outcome, visualizing it as vividly as possible. Reflect on how this visualization exercise can help reprogram your brain towards the desired change.

Write a letter to your future self, describing the person you want to become and the changes you want to make. Use specific language and vivid imagery to paint a clear picture of your desired transformation. Reflect on how this exercise can help reprogram your neural circuitry.

Practice mindfulness meditation for 10 minutes a day. Write down your experience and observations after each session, noting any shifts in your thought patterns or emotional states. Reflect on how this practice can support the rewiring of your brain.

Lesson 3:

Consistently practicing new thoughts and emotions rewires the brain, leading to lasting transformation.

Reflect on a negative thought pattern or emotional response that you would like to change. Write down three positive affirmations or empowering thoughts that counteract that pattern or response. Commit to repeating these affirmations daily to rewire your brain towards more positive thinking.

Keep a gratitude journal. Write down three things you are grateful for each day, focusing on specific details and emotions associated with each item. Reflect on how this practice can shift your neural circuitry towards more positive emotions and perceptions.

Engage in creative expression. Write down three different creative activities, such as painting, writing, or playing music, that you can incorporate into your routine. Reflect on how these activities can help rewire your brain by fostering new connections and stimulating different areas of your brain.

Chapter 4:
Meditation: Changing Your Mind and Brain

Lesson 1:

Meditation enables us to shift our focus from external distractions to our internal landscape.

Reflect on a recent situation where you felt overwhelmed or distracted by external factors. Write down the specific distractions and how they affected your state of mind. Reflect on how shifting your focus internally could have influenced your experience in that situation.

Create a list of three common external distractions or triggers that tend to pull you away from a focused and present state of mind. Write down alternative ways you can shift your focus internally when faced with these distractions to maintain a sense of calm and clarity.

Choose a daily activity that you often perform on autopilot, such as brushing your teeth or eating a meal. Write down three mindfulness techniques you can practice during this activity to bring your focus back to the present moment and cultivate a greater sense of awareness.

Lesson 2:

Through meditation, we can cultivate self-awareness, regulate emotions, and quiet the mind.

Take a few minutes to sit in a quiet space and focus on your breath. Afterward, write down any emotions or thoughts that arise during this brief meditation. Reflect on how this practice of observing your internal state can contribute to cultivating self-awareness and regulating emotions.

Choose one specific emotion that you often struggle with. Write down three meditation techniques or practices you can incorporate into your routine to help regulate and manage that emotion when it arises.

Reflect on a recent situation where your mind felt restless or cluttered with thoughts. Write down three meditation techniques, such as breath awareness or mantra repetition, that you can use to quiet your mind and enhance your ability to focus and concentrate.

Lesson 3:

Regular meditation practice supports neuroplasticity and helps break the habit of being ourselves.

Reflect on your current meditation practice, or if you're new to meditation, write about your motivations for starting a practice. Write down three specific benefits or changes you hope to experience through regular meditation practice.

Create a meditation schedule for the upcoming week. Write down the days and times you will dedicate to your practice. Reflect on how consistency and regularity in your meditation practice can support neuroplasticity and facilitate positive change.

_____

_____

_____

_____

_____

_____

_____

_____

_____

_____

_____

_____

_____

_____

_____

_____

_____

_____

_____

_____

_____

_____

_____

Write a journal entry after each meditation session, reflecting on any insights, shifts in mindset, or moments of clarity you experienced. Describe how these experiences contribute to breaking the habit of being yourself and support your overall well-being.

Chapter 5:
Deciding Who to Be

Lesson 1:

Our identity is not fixed; we have the power to decide who we want to be.

Take some time to reflect on your current identity and how it aligns with your authentic self. Write down three aspects of your identity that you would like to change or improve. Reflect on how embracing the power to decide who you want to be can create a sense of empowerment and transformation.

_____
_____
_____
_____
_____
_____
_____
_____
_____
_____
_____
_____
_____
_____
_____
_____
_____
_____
_____
_____
_____
_____
_____

Write a letter to your future self, describing the person you aspire to become. Be specific about the qualities, values, and behaviors you want to embody. Reflect on how this exercise of consciously choosing your desired identity can shape your thoughts, emotions, and actions.

Create a list of three affirmations or positive statements that reflect the identity you want to cultivate. Write them down and commit to repeating them daily. Reflect on how consistently affirming your desired identity can create a shift in your self-perception and over-all reality.

Lesson 2:

Making conscious choices aligned with our desired self creates a shift in our thoughts, emotions, and behaviors.

Reflect on a recent situation where you made a conscious choice that was aligned with your desired self. Write down the specific thoughts, emotions, and behaviors that arose as a result of that choice. Reflect on how this experience highlights the power of conscious decision-making in shaping your reality.

_____

_____

_____

_____

_____

_____

_____

_____

_____

_____

_____

_____

_____

_____

_____

_____

_____

_____

_____

_____

_____

_____

_____

Identify three specific areas of your life where you would like to see a shift in your thoughts, emotions, or behaviors. Write down three conscious choices you can make in each area to support that shift. Reflect on how these choices can create a cascading effect on your overall reality.

Write a journal entry at the end of each day, reflecting on the conscious choices you made throughout the day and how they aligned with your desired self. Describe any noticeable changes in your thoughts, emotions, or behaviors. Reflect on how this practice of conscious decision-making can lead to long-term transformation.

Lesson 3:

Clarifying our vision and purpose empowers us to embody our ideal self and manifest a new reality.

Take some time to reflect on your vision and purpose in life. Write down a clear and concise vision statement that encapsulates the reality you want to manifest. Reflect on how clarifying your vision can provide a sense of direction and empowerment.

Create a vision board or visual representation of your ideal self and the reality you want to manifest. Write a description of your vision board and how it aligns with your desired identity and reality. Reflect on how regularly engaging with this visualization practice can keep your vision and purpose at the forefront of your mind.

_____

_____

_____

_____

_____

_____

_____

_____

_____

_____

_____

_____

_____

_____

_____

_____

_____

_____

_____

_____

_____

_____

_____

Write a personal mission statement that outlines your purpose and values. Write down three action steps or commitments that you can make to live in alignment with this mission statement. Reflect on how embodying your purpose can empower you to make conscious choices that shape your desired reality.

Chapter 6:
Mind and Body

Lesson 1:

Our thoughts and emotions impact our physical health and well-being.

Reflect on a specific situation where your thoughts or emotions had a noticeable impact on your physical well-being. Write down the thoughts and emotions you experienced, and describe how they manifested in your body. Reflect on the connection between your mind and body in that situation.

_____
_____
_____
_____
_____
_____
_____
_____
_____
_____
_____
_____
_____
_____
_____
_____
_____
_____
_____
_____
_____
_____
_____
_____
_____

Choose a negative thought pattern or emotion that you would like to transform into a positive one. Write down three positive affirmations or empowering thoughts that counteract that pattern or emotion. Reflect on how adopting these new thoughts can positively impact your physical well-being.

Write a letter to your body, expressing gratitude and appreciation for its resilience and support. Acknowledge any negative thoughts or emotions you may have directed towards your body in the past, and commit to cultivating a more positive and loving relationship with it.

Lesson 2:

Practicing mindfulness and positive emotions promotes healing and overall well-being.

Create a daily gratitude journal. Write down three things you are grateful for each day, focusing on specific details and the emotions associated with each item. Reflect on how this practice of gratitude can promote healing and well-being in your life.

Choose one activity that you enjoy and that brings you positive emotions. Write down three ways you can incorporate this activity into your routine to enhance your overall well-being. Reflect on how regularly engaging in this activity can promote healing and positive emotions.

_____

_____

_____

_____

_____

_____

_____

_____

_____

_____

_____

_____

_____

_____

_____

_____

_____

_____

_____

_____

_____

_____

_____

_____

Practice a body scan meditation. Write down your experience and observations after each session, noting any physical sensations, areas of tension, or areas of ease. Reflect on how this practice of mindfulness can promote healing and a deeper connection between your mind and body.

Lesson 3:

By aligning our thoughts, emotions, and beliefs with our desired reality, we can experience profound physical transformations.

Reflect on a specific area of your physical health or well-being that you would like to transform. Write down three affirmations or positive statements that align with the desired reality you want to experience. Commit to repeating these affirmations daily and reflect on how they can contribute to your physical transformation.

Choose a limiting belief about your physical well-being that you want to release. Write down three empowering beliefs or statements that counteract that limitation. Reflect on how adopting these new beliefs can support your desired physical transformation.

_____

_____

_____

_____

_____

_____

_____

_____

_____

_____

_____

_____

_____

_____

_____

_____

_____

_____

_____

_____

_____

_____

_____

Write a visualization exercise where you vividly imagine yourself in a state of optimal physical health and well-being. Write a detailed description of how it feels, looks, and the actions you are engaged in. Reflect on how regularly engaging in this visualization exercise can align your thoughts, emotions, and beliefs with your desired physical reality.

_____

_____

_____

_____

_____

_____

_____

_____

_____

_____

_____

_____

_____

_____

_____

_____

_____

_____

_____

_____

_____

_____

Chapter 7:
Overcoming Your Environment and Body

Lesson 1:

Our external environment and internal beliefs can either support or hinder our transformation.

Reflect on your current external environment and its impact on your ability to make positive changes. Write down three specific elements of your environment that support your transformation, and three elements that hinder it. Consider how you can optimize your environment to better align with your goals.

Identify one self-limiting belief that has been holding you back from making desired changes. Write down three empowering beliefs or affirmations that counteract that limitation. Reflect on how adopting these new beliefs can support your transformation and reshape your internal environment.

Write a letter to your future self, describing the environment you envision for yourself and how it aligns with your goals and desired changes. Reflect on how consciously shaping your external environment can create a supportive and nurturing space for transformation.

Lesson 2:

Identifying and changing environmental triggers and self-limiting beliefs empowers us to break free from old patterns.

Reflect on a specific trigger in your environment that often leads to undesirable behaviors or habits. Write down three alternative responses or actions you can take when faced with that trigger, which align with your desired changes. Reflect on how these alternative responses can empower you to break free from old patterns.

Identify one self-limiting belief that has been holding you back from making a desired change. Write down three specific actions or experiences that challenge or counteract that belief. Reflect on how engaging in these actions or experiences can support your transformation and help you overcome the self-limiting belief.

Write a journal entry exploring the origins of one self-limiting belief you hold. Reflect on any experiences or influences that have contributed to the development of this belief. Write down three empowering perspectives or alternative beliefs that challenge and counteract the self-limiting belief.

Lesson 3:

Cultivating an empowering environment and mindset creates the conditions for sustainable change.

Reflect on your current mindset and how it influences your ability to make sustainable changes. Write down three empowering affirmations or positive statements that align with your desired changes. Commit to repeating these affirmations daily and reflect on how they contribute to cultivating an empowering mindset.

Create a vision board or visual representation of your empowering
environment and mindset. Write a description of your vision board
and how it aligns with your goals and desired changes. Reflect on
how regularly engaging with this visualization practice can create
the conditions for sustainable change.

_____

_____

_____

_____

_____

_____

_____

_____

_____

_____

_____

_____

_____

_____

_____

_____

_____

_____

_____

_____

_____

_____

Write a letter to a supportive person in your life, expressing your gratitude for their presence and their positive impact on your transformation. Reflect on how surrounding yourself with supportive individuals can contribute to an empowering environment and mindset.

Chapter 8:
Entering the Quantum Field

Lesson 1:

Our consciousness and intentions have a profound impact on the quantum field and the manifestation of our reality.

Reflect on a specific situation in your life where you believe your consciousness and intentions influenced the outcome. Write down three observations or experiences that support the idea that your thoughts and intentions shape your reality. Reflect on the power you hold in creating your own experiences.

Choose one specific intention or desired outcome that you want to manifest in your life. Write down three affirmations or positive statements that align with that intention. Commit to repeating these affirmations daily and reflect on how they contribute to tapping into the quantum field's creative potential.

Write a journal entry exploring your personal beliefs about the connection between consciousness and reality creation. Reflect on any limiting beliefs you may hold and write down three empowering beliefs that align with the idea that you have the power to shape your reality.

Lesson 2:

By aligning our thoughts, emotions, and beliefs with our desired reality, we tap into the quantum field's creative potential.

Choose a specific area of your life where you want to experience positive change. Write down three specific thoughts, emotions, or beliefs that are currently hindering your progress in that area. Reflect on how you can transform these hindering elements into thoughts, emotions, or beliefs that align with your desired reality.

Create a visualization exercise where you vividly imagine your-self living in alignment with your desired reality. Write a detailed description of how it feels, looks, and the actions you are engaged in. Reflect on how regularly engaging in this visualization exercise can support you in tapping into the quantum field's creative potential.

Write a letter to yourself, describing the person you are becoming as you align your thoughts, emotions, and beliefs with your desired reality. Reflect on how this exercise can reinforce your connection with the quantum field and increase your ability to manifest intentional change.

Lesson 3:

Developing a deep understanding of our interconnectedness and the universal field of energy supports our ability to create intentional change.

Reflect on a time when you felt a strong sense of interconnectedness with others or the world around you. Write down three specific experiences or observations that highlight this interconnectedness. Reflect on how developing a deeper understanding of this interconnectedness can support your ability to create intentional change.

Choose a specific practice or activity that helps you feel connected to the universal field of energy. Write down three ways you can incorporate this practice into your daily routine to deepen your understanding and connection. Reflect on how this practice can support your ability to create intentional change.

Write a journal entry exploring your beliefs about the universal field of energy and its influence on our reality. Reflect on any limiting beliefs you may hold and write down three empowering beliefs that align with the idea that you are connected to and can tap into this universal field of energy.

_____

_____

_____

_____

_____

_____

_____

_____

_____

_____

_____

_____

_____

_____

_____

_____

_____

_____

_____

_____

_____

_____

_____

_____

Chapter 9:
Tuning in to New Potentials

Lesson 1:

Expanding our awareness and embracing uncertainty opens up new possibilities for growth and transformation.

Write about a specific time in your life when you embraced uncertainty and expanded your awareness, leading to personal growth. Describe the situation, the challenges you faced, and how you overcame them. What did you learn from this experience? How did it transform you? What new possibilities opened up as a result?

Think about a current situation or challenge in your life where you feel stuck or uncertain. Write down three different perspectives or approaches you could take to address this situation. Consider how each perspective might open up new possibilities and potential outcomes. Reflect on the potential benefits and drawbacks of each perspective.

Identify an area of your life where you tend to stay within your comfort zone. Write about one specific action or step you can take to expand your awareness and embrace uncertainty in this area. Describe how you feel about this action and what potential new opportunities or growth it could bring. Commit to taking this action and write down a plan to implement it.

Lesson 2:

Practicing gratitude, openness, and curiosity helps us tune into new potentials and create transformative experiences.

Start a gratitude journal and write down three things you are grateful for each day. Reflect on why you are grateful for these things and how they contribute to your life. Notice any patterns or recurring themes in your gratitude journal and write about how these experiences or aspects have the potential to create transformative shifts in your perspective.

Choose a topic or subject that you have been curious about but haven't explored in depth. Write a list of questions you have about this topic and use online resources, books, or interviews to find answers. Reflect on how the process of exploring your curiosity expands your knowledge and opens up new potentials for growth and learning.

Think about a recent situation where you felt resistant or closed off to something new. Write about what caused your resistance and how it impacted your experience. Then, write a letter to yourself, expressing openness and willingness to embrace new experiences in the future. Reflect on how this shift in mindset could lead to transformative experiences and new potentials.

_____

_____

_____

_____

_____

_____

_____

_____

_____

_____

_____

_____

_____

_____

_____

_____

_____

_____

_____

_____

_____

_____

Lesson 3:

3. Letting go of attachments to specific outcomes allows for the emergence of greater possibilities in our lives.

Think about a specific goal or outcome you have been striving for. Write about why this goal is important to you and how it has been influencing your thoughts and actions. Then, explore the possibility of detaching from this specific outcome. Write down alternative possibilities or paths that could lead to even greater outcomes. Reflect on how letting go of attachment can open up new potentials and alleviate pressure.

Close your eyes and visualize yourself achieving a specific goal or outcome you desire. Allow yourself to fully experience the emotions associated with that achievement. Then, imagine letting go of that outcome and surrendering it to the universe or a higher power. Write about how this visualization exercise made you feel and the potential impact of releasing attachments to specific outcomes.

_____

_____

_____

_____

_____

_____

_____

_____

_____

_____

_____

_____

_____

_____

_____

_____

_____

_____

_____

_____

_____

_____

_____

Choose a recent situation or event where you had a specific outcome in mind. Write about the experience, including your thoughts, emotions, and actions leading up to it. Reflect on whether you were attached to a particular outcome and how that attachment influenced your experience. Write down three alternative outcomes that could have emerged from the situation, and consider the potential benefits of each. Reflect on how practicing mindfulness and letting go of attachment can lead to greater possibilities in your life.

_____

_____

_____

_____

_____

_____

_____

_____

_____

_____

_____

_____

_____

_____

_____

_____

_____

_____

_____

_____

_____

_____

Made in the USA
Las Vegas, NV
13 May 2024

89897881R00066